Outside in My Dressing Gown

and other poems for garden lovers

Outside In My Dressing Gown

...and other poems for garden lovers

Published in 2013 by

Bene Factum Publishing Ltd

PO Box 58122

London

SW8 5WZ

inquiries@bene-factum.co.uk

www.bene-factum.co.uk

ISBN: 978-1903071-96-0

A CIP catalogue record of this is available from the British Library

Cover design: Ian Hughes – Mousemat Design
Cover Illustration: Dorrance
Printed and bound in Malta for Latitude Press

Outside in My Dressing Gown

and other poems for garden lovers

by Liz Cowley

Cover illustration by Dorrance

For my family, all garden lovers, and with thanks
to my botanist friends Dr. John Akeroyd and Hugh
Synge for raking over my verse and weeding out
botanical inaccuracies.

Contents

AUTUMN

WINTER

SPRING

Season of hope, rebirth, new happiness

Where have you been hiding for so long?

So long coming –
a friend who doesn't call
or see you for months
until you despair.

I look out in the garden
remembering your company last year,
bringing me bunches of snowdrops,
crocus and jaunty, laughing daffodils.

You always come too late
and leave too early.
Why can't you arrive when I want you to?
Why do you always keep me waiting?

Spring –
where are you?
Where have you been hiding for so long?

Here at last

Season of hope, rebirth, new happiness,
with daffodils and snowdrops once again,
and gone at last, that wintry wilderness,
and mourning plants you've lost to frost and rain.
Season of fresh hope and new ambition,
with dreams of what to plant and what to do,
while picturing a gradual transition
as spring arrives and skies return to blue.
You step outside, you wander round the lawn,
your spirits lift, your garden is reborn.
Quite suddenly it soars – your disposition!

With buds now opening up before your eyes,
you feel a surge within your mental state
and do not trouble friends with winter sighs
or look within yourself and curse your fate.
Instead, you dream and plan what you'll be growing
in weeks to come now all the frost is gone,
and all the seeds you'll very soon be sowing –
at last empowered to smile, and carry on.
So long in coming, spring is here at last,
and even though the sky is overcast
the first new signs of life, at last, are showing.

A new spring in your step

One primrose, the first aconite,
one celandine, a single crocus –
one bloom can thrill, restore your will,
and bring a whole new sense of focus.

Wildly out of place

There's nothing that special about a wild garlic,
except the wild garlic once given to me.

A dear friend once dug it from some Sussex thicket,
it's now in my border, an odd place to be.

But there it keeps growing and sprouting each
springtime – and there it keeps spreading –
and year after year.

My friend is no longer. The garlic grows stronger,
and always reminds me of when he was here.

Butterfly

I am called a butterfly,
and very often wonder why
I wasn't called a 'flutter by',
describing how I pass you by.
In fact, each time I flutter by
I think the name of butterfly
was some unfortunate mistake –
it's such an easy one to make.
I dip and bob and flit a bit,
and dance and prance when in the air.
I should be called a 'flutter by'
describing how I'm flying there.

A flop

A hyacinth is great until
it's somehow gone and lost the will
to stay bolt upright in its pot,
and fades a shade and sags a lot.
You prop it up, and then despair
to see it wilting, tilting there.
It's sad to have to throw it out,
but who wants floppy plants about?
You stake it, do what you are able,
but still it droops upon the table,
as if it's somehow plunged in gloom
despite the fact it's still in bloom.
Too soon, before the flowers have died,
I give up, put the pot outside.
For me, it's not an indoor plant.
Put up with sagging blooms? I can't.

13

Gone

Where on earth are you?
Twenty years together,
and you fell out of my life,
just like that.

One day, you were there,
and the next you disappeared.
How could you?

You were my constant companion.
However hard things grew
you were always there for me –
sturdy, strong, solid,
easy to work with,
easy to be with.
And now you're in hiding.

I was a fool to lose you.
You fell out of my life suddenly,
leaving a gaping hole.

I have a replacement now,
but it's not the same.
I miss your strength,
your steeliness,
the touch and feel of you.

Where are you –
my favourite trowel?

Wallflowers

Wallflowers, in the wild such loners
who don't like company at all.
Colourful, but solitary,
content alone upon a wall.

Wallflowers, girls not asked to dance
and not content against the wall.
Unhappy, so unlike the flowers
who don't like any friends at all.

A giant mistake

A narrow door, a giant bamboo –
there's no way I could shove it through.
The back door is just three feet wide –
there's no chance it would go inside.

A garden centre is a pleasure,
but not if we don't take the measure
of shrubs and plants that catch our eye,
and then, in our excitement, buy.

I'm sure I'm not the only prat
to go and do exactly that.
Next time I'll have to use my eyes,
and, better, take the back door size.

I'm a cuckoo

I'm a cuckoo – 'Cuckoo!' 'Cuckoo!'
You sometimes hear me in the spring.
I never ever build a nest –
domestic work is not my thing.

I always find another nest
and then I pop an egg in there.
I'm sometimes guilty doing that.
Of course, I know it isn't fair.

But other birds will never guess.
It's odd – they never seem to know.
They're quite content to fetch the food
and see my baby cuckoo grow.

And what is more extraordinary –
they watch my fledgling growing stout,
and never seem to mind a bit
when my chick squeeezes all theirs out.

I leave them be. Well, that suits me.
That way, I can relax all spring,
and sit and laze upon a branch
while other birds do everything.

Who's cuckoo? Is it me or them?
I think I am a wise old bird.
Why rear your chicks when others will?
To me, that would be quite absurd.

An instant lift

Prozac lifts depression,
but flowers work better still.
It's good to keep some flowers
upon the windowsill.

A single bloom can comfort –
one golden daffodil
can lift one's mood in moments,
much faster than a pill.

I come down in the morning –
a flower above the sink
soon starts to raise my spirits,
and sometimes in a wink.

I start to boil the kettle
to make a cup of tea,
and every single morning
a flower smiles back at me.

No medic would prescribe that.
I would. I know a flower
can have a healing magic,
a special soothing power.

Especially in the morning,
and when the day is grey –
one bloom, one spot of colour
can chase the blues away.

Lettuces

The time I caught the gardening bug
was long ago, when I was seven,
and given a few lettuce seeds.
That summertime was utter heaven.

A single pack of Carter's seeds –
I think, perhaps, a birthday present.
Until that day I'd never guessed
that growing things could be so pleasant.

I sowed them out, I watched them grow
until I had a splendid show.
So clear remains that memory,
so many, many years ago.

Today I still remember eating
those splendid lettuces I grew.
What first gave you the gardening bug?
Do you remember, like I do?

Blackbird

Invited to the Sea of Colours,
the blackbird quarrelled with his mate.
Their argument went on for hours,
and then the poor chap turned up late.

By now all other birds had been –
alas, there were no colours left.
The blackbird cried and flew off home,
still black and utterly bereft.

But then God saw and pitied him,
and made a sudden kindly choice,
'Dear blackbird', said the Lord to him,
'instead, you'll have the finest voice.

Too late for colours, that's a shame.
You could have done with one or two.
Instead, I'll let you sing a song
and like no other bird can do.'

And that explains why blackbirds sing
in notes so soft and sweet and low,
and pour their hearts out when they sing,
quite unlike other birds you know.

God, that's embarrassing!

God does have taste, and lots of it,
but sometimes he slipped up a bit
designing rude and naughty flowers –
perhaps it's his idea of wit.

Some species seem to have erections
and frilly, all too female sections,
while cacti can be most alarming
with bits I often find disarming.

But still, the rudest plants on earth
suggest he has a certain mirth
and likes to hear a bit of laughter –
both here, and in the world thereafter.

The belles of the ball

Bluebells – nothing like them,
a sea beneath a tree.
A dell beneath the beeches –
a favourite sight for me.

A stroll amidst the bluebells
quite takes my breath away.
What other belles beat bluebells?
They always make my day.

But how can people steal them?
I can't believe it's true
that people often do that.
I never would, would you?

No, if you're a gardener.
I'm pretty sure that's true.
Plant lovers couldn't do that –
the last thing they would do.

You gaze beneath the beech trees
and see a swathe of blue.
But others see a fortune –
and often make one, too.

A roof terrace

You picture a roof terrace:
pots, a table, chairs and friends.
But will the rooftop take the weight?
That can be where the dreaming ends.

It's sensible to check the deeds
and see if you can get permission.
Though sadly, if the house is old,
it could be an unsafe transition.

The roof was used for hanging washing
and not for summer entertaining.
Go ahead without permission,
and soon the joists might start complaining.

Most roofs were used for access only,
and not for having people there,
or planting, paving, soil, foundations,
and tubs and pots placed everywhere.

Warning – get a good surveyor!
Of course, the cost will be a drag.
But surely it is best to know
your renovated roof won't sag?

You've got permission!

At last you've got the go-ahead!
Your rooftop garden's on its way –
but what will grow and thrive up there
with sunshine blazing down all day?

Choose plants from Oz, the Middle East,
or California or the Med,
or something South American.
Most British plants will soon be dead.

Grasses also love it hot,
but do take care how tall they grow!
Too tall, and bits of them may blow
upon pedestrians below.

Ground cover? Try Elijah Blue.
It's so at home with glass or steel.
It's funky, fierce electric blue
and gives your roof a modern feel.

Dwarf conifers and lavenders
and herbs will all adore it there.
Imagine – rosemary, lemon balm
and thyme scents floating everywhere!

At last, you've got the go-ahead.
At last your rooftop's on its way.
It's time to think of what to plant,
and open that champagne today!

Digging deep

'A way to whistle through your money?
Just fall in love with trees and plants.'
I wish I'd listened to my mother.
I should have listened to my aunts.

How true it was! How true it is!
Thank God I don't have that much space.
I hate to think what I would spend
if planting out a larger place.

'A way to whistle through your money?
A garden, dear!' How true, how true,
as even in a little patch, you spend too much.
At least, I do.

Health and stupidity

Great tree,
that sang like the sea,
and freckled and speckled the street
with shimmering shadows.
Great tree,
history,
condemned by the council
because of conkers.
Bonkers.

Health, safety, insanity.
How could you ever chop that tree?

No more griefs allayed
under the calm of your whispering canopy,
no more leaves to catch in autumn,
or white spires heralding spring.
No more conkers.
Bonkers.

Great tree,
history,
now felled by those too blind to see
your beauty,
their stupidity.

Now scrawled across its stump
'Why me?'

A sad tail

A baby squirrel, lovely sight,
the memory still makes me wail –
the bloody cat was chasing it,
attracted by its bushy tail.

The squirrel ran, the poor wee thing,
and found a hole within a tree.
One bite, and what an awful sight –
the cat then brought its tail to me.

The tail, of course, was sticking out –
the cat thought it a perfect present.
Of all the gifts I've ever had
that had to be the most unpleasant.

Tree of heaven

I have a tree of heaven,
it's called 'the widow's tree'.
It's dangerous to climb it –
the branches fall, you see.

Most will not support you –
they snap off now and then,
and sadly, they have ended
the lives of several men.

I have a tree of heaven –
it's forty metres high.
It costs a bomb to prune it;
so dangerous, that's why.

One day, it may well kill me.
In fact, I know it will –
next time they come to lop it
and when I pay the bill.

Guilt

Insecticides and pesticides,
and pellets to keep off the slugs,
and fertilizers on the lawn
and sprays to kill off mites and bugs,
and compost bags containing peat,
so much that's not environmental –
this year, I'll try to be more gentle.

Nails

Pet hate among my garden loves –
ten broken nails. But garden gloves
don't let you feel how plants are growing,
or quite which way their roots are going.
I'd love to grow both nails and plants.
Impossible – no bloody chance.

Tulipomania, Holland, 1630s

Imagine – a large house, swapped for a tulip!
Quite common in Holland a long time ago.
Numerous houses were swapped for prize tulips,
the best of the bulbs that they managed to grow.

One Amsterdam mansion facing the river
was swapped for a bulb in the biggest transaction,
and history records that buyer and seller
concluded the deal with great satisfaction.

One bulb was swapped for a cellar of cheese –
one thousand pounds of it! Four oxen, too,
and eight pigs as well, plus a suit and a bed.
All that's recorded; amazing but true.

One poor old Dutchman swallowed a tulip –
he thought that the bulb was an onion, you see.
The bulb nearly killed him, as did the knowledge
he'd swallowed a fortune while eating his tea.

'Tulipomania' turned people mental,
and when the bubble eventually burst,
Holland's economy crashed – a disaster –
with bulb speculators vilified, cursed.

Who'd swap a house for a bulb? Well, the Dutch did.
The records all show it is perfectly true.
It's hard to believe it, or even conceive it.
What crazy, what mad things plant lovers can do!

The jay – a true story

A frail old lady lived next door
who needed heart pills every day –
a dose of six on waking up,
or else she would have passed away.

Her carer always laid them out
upon her bedroom windowsill –
a line of six, all shiny bright,
to stop my neighbour getting ill.

One day a hungry jay flew in
and swallowed them, yes, every one,
delighted with their rainbow shades
all glinting in the morning sun.

Alas, he fainted, dropped to earth,
and fell into a flowerbed.
The carer looked out, horrified,
assuming that he must be dead.

By chance, the RSPCA
was only fifty yards away.
The lady lived, I'm glad to say –
and so, I'm thankful, did the jay.

When I get ill and need a pill,
I've learned my lesson; so have they –
the frail old lady next to us,
the carer – and, of course, the jay.

Latin

The classes you sat in
to do all that Latin –
forgotten: each word that you heard.
With plant names in Latin,
the classes you sat in
were not, perhaps, quite as absurd.

Why is the willow weeping?

The willow weeps,
the willow cries,
it longs to be an upright tree,
not drooping down towards the earth
and weeping so lamentably.

The willow weeps,
the willow grieves,
it yearns to be an upright tree
with branches stretched towards the sun,
not weeping there in misery.

A high rise flat

A shoebox? Tiny balcony?
Fix window boxes on the ledge,
and plant some trailers like nasturtiums –
they'll soon shoot off across the edge.
It's nice for you, and great for us
when looking up from way below.
It puts a spring within our step
and makes us smile before we go.

SUMMER

I'm outside in my dressing gown –
I often am at half past seven

Summer

Now comes the season for a lunch outside,
a jug of Pimms, with friends and neighbours there,
and gorgeous plants and flowers on every side
and fragrances and birdsong in the air.
And here's the best excuse for never cooking.
Why bother during pleasant salad days?
At last the perfect time for simply lazing –
you've done the planting; just sit back and gaze.
What better time of year for entertaining –
to eat outside, without it always raining?
Just strolling round your garden is amazing!

Failing flowers

I don't want to know you,
because I can't grow you –
I've done what I can
and you're ailing.
You don't like my garden?
My heart starts to harden
if I do my best
and you're failing.

Picnics

Lovely thought, til someone's stung
or skids into a pile of dung;

lovely thought, with skies of blue –
until they start to rain on you;

lovely thought, until your chair
collapses, and beyond repair;

lovely thought, the food you've done –
until it's melted by the sun;

(it's not that long before its rays
will spoil your home-made mayonnaise)

lovely thought, but not that mileage,
or picnicking with smells of sileage;

lovely when you've found a view,
though that can take an hour or two.

The very best lunch spot to be?
Your garden! Well, it is for me.

Outside in my dressing gown

I'm outside in my dressing gown –
I often am at half past seven,
when plants are sometimes waking up.
To me, that is a time of heaven.

The builders on the roof next door
were once surprised to see me there,
amazed to watch me pottering
in slippers and with unbrushed hair.

Thank God they've learned to look away,
accepting there's a nut next door
who's up and out and not yet dressed –
they don't look startled any more.

They do their own thing, I do mine –
they glance at me, then look away.
I'm glad they have accepted it –
the way I like to start the day.

I know I'm not a rarity

Linda is a dawn dead-header –
like me, she's out in slippered feet.
Her garden's open to the public –
by nine o'clock, it must look neat.

Cyd's an early morning dibber,
by seven, plucking daisies out.
She likes to get out there first thing,
at dawn – with no-one else about.

Prue's into plants that soothe and heal –
she's studied homeopathy.
She, too, is often out at dawn
and wandering contentedly.

Jacqui is an early riser,
she doesn't like to lounge in bed.
Not when she could be in her garden
and sipping coffee there instead.

I know that there are many thousands
of dressing gowners just like me,
outside, and dibbing, snipping, brushing –
I know I'm not a rarity.

Ground elder

Disaster! Roots just like spaghetti.
You dig them up, then swear a bit.
Ground elder always comes to stay.
You know you won't get rid of it.

Spaghetti roots are everywhere.
You dig them up, and bitterly.
You know you've got enough out there
to cover half of Italy.

Spaghetti roots – impossible –
and most of them you can't remove.
So if ground elder's in your place,
there's only one solution. Move!

Suburban lament

Where have all front gardens gone?
Long time passing.
Where have all front gardens gone?
Long time ago.
Where have all front gardens gone?
Under cars, and every one.
When will we ever learn?
When will we ever learn?

Where have all the flowers gone?
Long time passing.
Where have all the borders gone?
Long time ago.
Where have shrubs and hedges gone?
Under carports, every one.
When will we ever learn?
When will we ever learn?

Where have all the raindrops gone?
Long time pouring.
Where have all the raindrops gone?
Long time ago.
Where have all the raindrops gone?
Flooding gutters every one.
When will we ever learn?
When will we ever learn?

With apologies to Pete Seeger and his poignant song,
'Where have all the flowers gone?'

A ballad about a salad

Nasturtium petals in a salad?
It seems a rather nice idea,
though men will always pick them out,
at least the chaps invited here.

The sight of petals in a salad
is something fellows cannot take,
and soon they start to pick them out
as if they fell in by mistake.

They look at them, all quizzical.
Astonished, they then look at you
and wonder if they're edible.
They never quite know what to do.

Flowers are flowers and lettuce, lettuce,
and men will always wonder whether
you've flipped and gone right off your head
when serving up the two together.

My sister's complaint

'What idiot would want a pool?
I did, and what a bloody fool.
You picture it – a pool out there,
with friends and family everywhere.

You say it's healthy, good for you
to have a daily swim or two.
The truth is pools are lots of work
which other people always shirk.

You put out chairs – they leave them there.
They watch you tidy everywhere.
They bring out towels – you take them back.
They sunbathe – you keep things on track.

You make them drinks on summer days
and sandwiches and canapés.
They eat, they drink – and then they laze
while you are clearing up the trays.

And no-one ever quite believes
the time it takes to dredge the leaves,
or what it costs to heat or clean
or stop the water going green.

You're always netting, trawling, skimming,
and never have the time for swimming.
What idiot would want a pool?
I guess I'm not the only fool.'

Battleground

I am in command of an army.
There are enemies everywhere
clustering on the borders,
waiting to strangle or suffocate silently,
creep up on my troops unawares
and little by little eat away at our numbers.
I am on constant guard.

I inspect my platoons regularly,
supply them with good rations,
talk to and encourage them,
select those for the front,
demote them if necessary
and weed out the weakest.

They do well because I look after them,
make sure they work together as a team
and want them to triumph.

It is a constant battle looking after my garden.

Living with Leylandii

Leylandii, stop growing!
You're blocking out the light –
too dense and dark and stifling;
I hate your mighty height.

The kitchen's plunged in darkness.
So, too, the sitting room.
Small wonder that my spirits
are mired in gloom and doom.

Leylandii too near you
is frequently depressing.
No light, no pleasant blooms in sight –
oppressive and distressing.

I can't believe how neighbours
can plant them, think them splendid,
while blocking light and view from you
until your friendship's ended.

Dragonflies

About to leave my house one day
I heard a tapping noise again,
and saw a dragonfly enmeshed
in cobwebs on the window pane.
I fetched a ladder, lunged my hand
amidst the webs – the spider fled –
and took the lovely creature down.
The flapping stopped – yet was he dead?

But then I stroked each silky strand
from both of his entangled wings.
He also tried to free himself
of all his ropes and sticky strings.
I stayed with him a good two hours –
I had to wait 'til he was free,
and knew I'd make my uncle cross
arriving two hours late for tea.

At last he fluttered, braced himself,
and finally he flew away.
What joy it was to see him go!
I never will forget that day.
And better still, he flew right back
and circled round me once or twice.
Was that a thankyou? Who can tell?
But thinking that was rather nice.

I love all dragonflies today,
and watching them is utter bliss –
especially when they soar away.
I always feel a heartbeat miss.

Wasp-watching

Ever watched a wasp eat ham?
It's far preferred to any jam.
They chop a chunk upon your plate,
then try and take too great a weight
to others waiting in the nest,
clutched tightly underneath the chest.
They often wobble as they go,
and drop the precious load below.

A large and tasty chunk of ham
is far preferred to any jam
or marmalade spread on your toast.
It's clear that wasps love ham the most.

Just listen when they leave your table!
They buzz as loudly as they're able.
It makes them heroes of the day –
they know it as they fly away.
Ham gives all wasps a splendid buzz –
you hear it, and you know it does.

Nature's a demanding boss

A gardener's work is never done –
it lasts until the day you drop.
There's always a new job to do,
and usually, four more on top.

Nature's a demanding boss
who's always asking more of you –
a tough and unforgiving sort
who loves to push and challenge you.

She's not the same from day to day,
and even changes hour to hour.
You never can rely on her.
No other boss exerts such power.

Nature's a demanding boss,
so fickle, moody and capricious.
She can be kind to you at times,
but equally, she can be vicious.

Nature's a tough boss alright,
until you're somewhere six feet under.
She'll always pile more work on you,
but millions love her – that's the wonder.

An unholy alliance

God never talks to me when in cathedrals.
He pauses where I sit, then walks on by.
My ears are deaf, my thoughts on architecture –
the vaults and pillars stretching to the sky.

God does not talk to me in country churches,
He used to once; no longer does he try.
In fact, he never talks to me in buildings.
I've come at last to know exactly why.

He only ever speaks to me in gardens,
and when I gaze with awe at plants and flowers.
Who made such lovely things? I always wonder.
And then he sometimes talks to me for hours.

God has no time for me in holy places,
but sometimes he is there for me outside,
talking to me gently as I garden –
somehow a soothing presence at my side.

At christenings, funerals, weddings, any service,
I do not talk to God, nor he to me.
We do not have a comforting communion –
he glances at me, then he leaves me be.

But maybe in a graveyard I will hear him,
if primroses and daffodils are there,
or purple violets growing round a gravestone
and fragrances around me in the air.

An atheist I'm not, but just a doubter,
except at times, when in an outside space,
surrounded by the miracles of nature.
It's only then we talk – the only place.

Moving

Prioritise the garden,
if no back door is there.
Or else, invite a houseful
of mud, crud, everywhere.

Our neighbours quite forgot that
and lugged the plants inside,
then out into the garden.
The mess! Oh, how they cried!

They even brought cement in
to mend the garden wall,
and then, of course, the bags split
when dragged into the hall.

The worst thing is their carpets –
once cream, they're turned to brown.
It cost a bomb to buy them,
and then to lay them down.

Never do a house up
until the garden's done,
unless it has good access.
If not, it isn't fun.

Snails

It's time I learned to stamp on snails,
not throw them over walls.
Each time I throw, the guilt won't go
as each poor creature falls.

Quite dead on impact? Hard to tell.
The shell is smashed for sure.
But just how long does each survive?
Ten minutes? Maybe more.

If I were born a humble snail,
I'd like a kinder end,
not have my house smashed into me
as soon as I descend.

I think each knows the end is nigh –
retracting in its shell.
I'm sure they know before you throw
that all is far from well.

Each time I chuck a wretched snail,
I hear a horrid crack,
and then regret my cruelty,
too late for turning back.

I'll have to learn to stamp on them –
that's something I must do.
But how I'd hate the gooey mess
stuck underneath my shoe.

I've smashed a load of gastropods –
a thousand, maybe more.
If God loves snails, he won't love me,
of that I can be sure.

And God himself might be a snail
and take one look at me,
and throw me out, or into hell
for all eternity.

Ugh!

Slugs – the nastiest of bugs,
each one a spineless jelly blob.
There's something ugh about a slug –
thank God those pellets do their job.
But how I hate those melting blobs
I find at dawn around each pot,
and picking, flicking each one off
is not a task I like a lot.

Summer in the country

The bull rushes out, the cow slips about,
and thousands of wasps are arriving.
The sunshine is bringing a host of things stinging,
and millions of insects are thriving.

The plants are all shooting, the dragons are snapping,
and adders are adding to numbers,
and just when you're dozing in bed in the morning,
a mower then ruins your slumbers.

The rooks are all sawing with deafening cawing –
hardly a sound that's enthralling.
With buzz saws and tractors, among other factors,
the noise is quite often appalling.

The tourists are heaving, you soon feel like leaving
when beautiful gardens are showing.
The cost of the parking, the crowding and queuing
can easily put you off going.

The sun can be boiling and very soon spoiling
a picnic or day at the sea.
Wherever you're going, the traffic is slowing,
and a one-hour trip turns into three.

What's equally jarring is smells of meat charring
and wafting from gardens next door.
What everyone's doing – of course, barbecuing.
They think that's what summer is for.

The summer's delightful, but often quite frightful
with crowds and the noise and the stinging.
It's best to keep gazing at what is amazing,
forgetting the downsides it's bringing.

Nightmare

The foxes are dating, and noisily mating,
and now what's the chance of your sleeping?
With courtship about, all sleeping is out
until your alarm clock is bleeping.

The foxes are mating; it's so irritating –
that screaming and wailing and sighing.
The noise is a curse, and what's even worse,
it sounds like a child who is dying.

It sounds just like murder.
The female – you've heard her?
A terrible sound in the night.
You won't sleep 'til morning,
until the day's dawning.
You won't get a wink 'til first light.

A growing mystery

What is it that makes dahlias grow
in other gardens that I see,
and often so prolifically –
yet makes them wilt and die on me?

Why can't I ever grow a hosta
that doesn't end up full of holes
when loads of other people can?
That's still among my gardening goals.

Why is it that my clematis
appears to struggle every year,
and after all I've done for it?
Why do some plants not like it here?

Why can't I even grow sweet peas?
Sweet peas are never sweet to me.
They soon go grey and wilt away
while most folk grow them easily.

It's not the soil – I've tested that.
It's not for want of TLC.
It's not for want of anything.
There must be something wrong with me.

It's lucky that I'm not the type
to suffer pangs of jealousy,
but why do flowers grow for others
and then refuse to grow for me?

Rambling Rector

Rambling Rector,
Rambling Rector,
what a splendid, gorgeous rose!
I marvel at its mass of blooms
and at the speed at which it grows!

Racing Rector,
Racing Rector,
it races all around a tree!
Its size – you can't believe your eyes,
or how it grows so speedily!

And then it goes and sheds its blossoms,
refusing to come out again.
The Rector's an annoying chap –
a joy at first, too soon a pain.

Quite lovely for a month or two,
but then a tangled mess out there –
a mass of boring foliage
with petals littered everywhere.

Are you named after a flower?

So many, many flower names
are always heaped on womankind.
But boys with any flower names?
That's something that you never find.
Except for Basil. Why not Mint?
And what is wrong with Chive, or Sage?
That's perfect for a little chap
who's clever for his tender age.
And why no tree names for the lads
like Pine or Oak or even Cedar?
A good strong name like that at birth
suggests a wise and future leader.
But think of all the female names
from gardens, fields, and lanes and forests!
It's almost as if baby girls
have turned their parents into florists.

Hyacinth, Hazel, Rose and Violet,
Erica and Mirabelle,
Aster, Flora, Myrtle, Daisy,
Genista, Fern and Asphodel,
Pansy, Primrose, Ivy, Lily,
Marigold, Azalea, Scilla,
Veronica and May and Heather,
Laurel, Holly, Alchemilla,
Viola, Poppy, Daphne, Willow,
Zinnia, Cherry and Nigella,
Rosamunda, Amaryllis,
Saffron, Jasmine, Rosabella,
Honeysuckle, Sorrel, Jasmine,
Nerine, Zebrina, Honesty,

Calla, Vera, Pink, Viola,
Rosy, Posy, Bryony,
Hebe, Lavender and Iris,
Lilac, busy Lizzie, May –
does everyone read gardening books
before the infant's naming day?
Rosemary of course, and Hazel,
Virginia – it goes on and on.
They must be reading loads of books,
to find a name to hit upon.

It's clear why Hogwort's not a choice,
and Deadly Nightshade wouldn't do,
but why no spud or veggie names?
I think we miss a trick or two.
Maris Piper – what a name!
Courgette is rather stylish too,
and with a name like Cauliflower,
the whole world would remember you.

A south-facing garden

South means sun, and lots and lots,
and colour, colour in your pots.
But facing south can mean the sun
can blaze all day, oppressing one.

And many plants don't like hot sun,
unless they're species from the Med,
or else South Africa or Oz,
or South America instead.

Best not to introduce a plant
that cannot take a bit of drought.
And if it's raining, mulch a bit,
but never when the sun is out.

Callistemon will be contented.
Geraniums will love it there,
as will Campsis, Regal Lilies –
they love the sunshine everywhere..

South-facing? Bit too hot for me.
I'd rather mine were facing west.
But many happy gardeners
think south is nicer, quite the best.

Drought intolerant

Delphiniums, Pansies, Primulas,
Impatiens, Lobelia,
plants in baskets and in pots,
Dicentras and Begonia –
all of them will start to grump
as soon as they are starved of water.
You need to keep any eye on them,
or else their lives will be much shorter.

Mowing

My chap's a straight liner.
He thinks nothing's finer
than mowing at ninety degrees.
I don't much like mowing
or lines that are showing,
or mowing the bits round the trees.

While he does the mowing
I get on with sowing –
he doesn't like planting, you see.
A happy estrangement,
him mowing, me sowing –
the perfect arrangement for me.

Water, water everywhere,
and not a drop that's free

You've been away on holiday –
two weeks abroad, and back today.
The gardener's not turned off the hose,
and now what will you have to pay?

You work it out, one visit only,
and that was seven days ago.
Good God! One week of pouring water!
At least two hundred pounds or so.

Days and days of pouring water –
the grass is dazzling – emerald green –
and half the garden's now a lake.
But make him pay? You can't. That's mean.

You go inside and pour a drink,
and wish you hadn't been away.
You may as well buy water lilies
and plant them on the lawn today.

Allotment wars

Someone's dug up Bill's potatoes
in yet another nightly raid,
and stolen all of Stanley's plums
and even nicked Amanda's spade,
and dug up Bertie's giant pumpkin
(the one that he was due to show)
as well as taking all Jim's carrots,
along with his new fork and hoe.
And worse, they all suspect each other
(though feeling guilty that they do).
A common story in allotments.
Today, it's all too often true.

In one allotment that I know
a policeman hid within a tree –
poor chap, compelled to stay all night
to find out who the thief could be.
And did the culprit ever show?
Of course not, with the crops all gone.
Amazing what the police will do
and waste the public's money on.
I like the concept of allotments,
but not the stories that I hear
of people nicking plants and veg,
and fruits and tools that disappear,
or folks who think they run the place,
and style themselves 'allotment king',
while telling others what to do
and making rules for everything.

Hollyhocks

Do rust if you must,
but not in my plot.
The first sign of rust and I'm fuming.
The very first spot –
you're out on the dot,
and whether or not you are blooming.

Some people aren't fussed
by hollyhock rust –
they look at the blossoms instead.
But I hate the spots
and blotches and dots,
and rust is a sight that I dread.

The plants I can't trust
to live without rust
will not have a place on my plot.
I think it looks grotty
when plants go all spotty
and leaves look decidedly shot.

Talking to vegetables

You come outside and talk to us –
you think that helps to make us grow.
You touch our leaves and say nice things
while walking up and down our row.

We grow for you, we put on weight –
your words are most encouraging,
and then when we are large and strong,
you do a most appalling thing.

You chop us down, you cut us up,
you boil us up and then you eat us,
and after all we've done for you.
How could you cheat and so mistreat us?

What kind of soul is it?

It has to be a troubled kind of soul
who takes no solace in our plants and flowers,
and never thinks to fill a vase or bowl,
or runs or walks each week for several hours,
but does not notice plants where they are going,
and gets through many months – or just one day –
oblivious to everything that's growing,
quite unaware of blooms upon their way.
Denied the pleasure of our plants and flowers
and breathing in their scents and soothing powers
their problems must be truly overflowing.

Herbaceous borders

Herbaceous borders? Great until
they start to make a moan of it,
and dry and sigh, and ask you why
you haven't gone and done your bit.

Such borders – nice, until the day
they groan that they are starving, drying,
especially if you've been away
and left them hungry, thirsty, dying.

All lovely for a little while,
but all too often they're complaining
you never do enough for them,
or grumping that it's not been raining.

They're mostly days and days of work,
and needing constant, constant weeding,
or filling in or thinning out,
or hoeing, pruning or reseeding.

I wish they were contented things,
instead of critics, dreadful moaners,
resenting you at every turn
and wishing that you weren't their owners.

Large borders – now too much for me.
Like children, they are far too needy.
Too hungry, thirsty, too demanding.
And, above all, far too weedy.

Favourite view

A lovely sight within a garden –
a friendly chap who does your mowing,
and fetches ladders, climbs up trees
and prunes them when they're overgrowing,
and does the things that you don't want to –
like weeding, clearing up and hoeing,
and helps you with the heavy work,
and recognizes what you're growing.

The nicest sight within a garden –
a willing fellow, tall and strong,
who does the jobs you ask him to
and never ever takes too long.
A splendid sight within your garden,
as nice as any plant or flower –
an honest chap who helps you out
and doesn't charge too much an hour.

Hedgehog

I find a baby hedgehog –
a tiny ball, newborn,
alone without his mother,
curled up upon the lawn.

I try and find his mother
to reunite the pair,
and spot the nest quite quickly
and place the babe back there.

But then, ten minutes later,
he's on the lawn again,
and this time, he's been bitten
and obviously in pain.

There's no way I can help him –
too late. I watch him die.
A tiny babe, abandoned.
I often wonder why.

A helples newborn hedgehog,
so cruelly rejected,
and left to die a second time –
that's not what I expected.

A west-facing garden

West, the best! At least, for me.
Not too hot, and not too cold.
On one side, bright and colourful,
the other greener, not as bold.

Never hammered by strong sunlight,
or else cold winds, a place of dreams –
since facing west, most plants will thrive,
except the ones that like extremes.

Often bathed in dappled sunshine
with trees protecting plants below.
West is best. At least, I think so –
the best position that I know.

Foxgloves

Foxgloves, what heartwarming plants
with gloves to put upon your fingers!
Each time I see a foxglove now,
that childhood memory always lingers.

Fuchsias

Fuchsia blooms – like ballerinas
in tutus, dancing all day long
as soon as there's the slightest breeze
or when a high wind comes along.

A corps de ballet on each bush,
a mass of dancers – heavenly!
They're always great performers, fuchsias,
and get a huge encore from me.

Fuchsias, artistes, ballet stars –
more lovely than most plants I know.
On breezy days I step outside
and then sit back and watch the show.

The language of flowers

When entertaining Orientals,
be careful when arranging flowers.
Lots of Eastern folk are mystics
and think that flowers have special powers.

Some flowers say 'Welcome', others don't,
and how they're placed and what you choose
can send out different messages
depending on their shapes and hues.

You go outside and pick some flowers
while picturing a nice arrangement.
Beware, without a bit of care
your vase might lead to long estrangement.

They step inside, they see your vase,
and not long after, they've departed.
You ask yourself, 'What have I done?'
and that's before the evening's started.

Some plants suggest an ancient grievance
and several may offend their eyes,
or even prompt deep gasps of shock
suggesting someone's swift demise.

You go and pick a bunch of flowers
and pop them in a vase or pot,
while thinking it will welcome them.
The chances are that it may not.

An east-facing garden

The hardest type, most difficult,
in winter cool, in summer dry.
And early sunshine clobbers plants,
and all too often, favourites die.

Harsh morning sun will burn the leaves –
you soon see foliage complaining
when trapped beneath its gaze and blaze,
especially if it's been raining.

The secret is to buy the plants
that thrive in most north-facing spaces.
That way, a garden facing east
can be the loveliest of places.

Antirrhinums

Press a bloom; a mouth comes open,
and then pretend it speaks to you.
Have a moment's conversation,
exactly like you used to do.

Press the blooms, then talk to them,
create what they say back to you.
Another precious memory,
and still a lovely thing to do.

For Ray and Onya

Ray owned a splendid railway
that ran right round the floor.
He even built a tunnel
within the kitchen door.

But Onya didn't like it –
she longed to have a place
with trains not running round it
and taking up the space.

They bought a place in Ireland,
Ray put the tracks outside.
Now trains steam round the garden,
and how poor Onya cried!

She can't grow any flowers
much more than inches high,
or else they block the tracks up
and stop trains getting by.

She can't grow things with petals
or leaves that wilt or drop,
or tall things like delphiniums
in case the steam trains stop.

She can't plant any bushes –
they'd all grow far too tall,
or favourites like azaleas –
in case the blossoms fall.

Her garden back in London
made Onya very proud.
Now all the plants she loved there
are simply not allowed.

The grandchildren love coming –
that's helped to save the day,
they love the model railway
each time they come and stay.

But Onya's still not happy
with plants so low and small.
She thinks the railway's stunning.
The garden? Not at all.

Chelsea Flower Show

Too many allowed in,
too much overcrowding,
with most people taller than me.
If you can't see the prizes
and all the surprises,
I think you should get in for free.

What's the point of you going
if you can't see what's showing,
and stuck in a crowd that's so tall?
If you can't see the flowers
and you're crammed there for hours,
what's the point of you going at all?

If you can't see exhibits,
it somewhat inhibits
the thrill and excitement of going.
If you're six foot or taller
that's fine – but if smaller,
don't go there; you need to keep growing.

What's more, I loathe trekking
to see all that decking,
and gardens with sculptures in steel.
Like most folk, I'm keener
on gardens much greener,
and those with a natural feel.

What's the point of a ticket,
if then you can't stick it
and all you can see is a crowd?
I find it a pain, and I won't go again –
such numbers should not be allowed.

The one day, and best day
to go is the Press Day,
when numbers are very much lower.
You stroll at your leisure,
the show is a pleasure,
and there's time to meet up with a grower.

If armed with a press pass,
you're treated as first class,
and better, to flutes of champagne.
Without one, it's less fun,
the crowding annoys one.
I don't think I'll go there again.

Hampton Court Flower Show

So very different, Hampton Court –
the space to gaze and stroll around,
with plants and Pimms and picnic spaces
and covering so much more ground.

So much less stressful, Hampton Court –
a thousand lovely things to view,
while never jammed within a crowd
or queue that almost crushes you.

The River Thames, a gentle pace,
a splendid place in which to roam
and spot that stunning, gorgeous plant,
and then, with joy, to take it home.

Sissinghurst

'Rooms outside' – a lovely thought –
so calming is it for the soul
when house and garden blend like that
and work together as a whole.

'A white room', also beautiful,
no other colours in the space –
a garden that so soothes the mind;
pure heaven, such a tranquil place.

A garden with a flow to it,
a series there of smooth transitions,
from room to room with plants to view
in perfectly thought out positions.

The garden I'd most love to own,
or wander in, or visit first?
I know the one that it would be.
Where else but lovely Sissinghurst?

Swallow's nest

A nest, and right above our door –
they're back – the swallows – same place, dammit!
And now, each time we go outside,
we tell each other not to slam it.

We often do – the parents fly,
and leave the fledglings on their own,
and then we fear they won't return
with chicks too young to cope alone.

'Don't slam that door!' we always say
each time we need to go outside.
The trouble it, it doesn't shut
unless we slam it – though we've tried.

My husband cannot use the plane –
the scraping sounds would soon alarm them
and scare the parents off again.
We wouldn't ever want to harm them.

Please, swallows, find another home,
and swallows, dearest, what is more,
we don't like having droppings there
each time we step outside the door.

A north-facing garden

Many people soon despair
when faced with a north-facing space.
But lots of plants will be contented.
For plenty, it's the perfect place.

You may complain about the shade,
but several stunning plants don't care –
ferns and hostas, they'll both love it,
and skimmias will do well there.

And, if there is little sunlight,
gooseberries, cherries are for you,
and epidemium loves shade
and gives you great ground cover too.

Plus garrya will be quite happy,
content against a shady wall.
No reason to hide tools away,
no reason, none, to cry at all!

Buddleia and butterflies

Some plants are quite extraordinary,
My buddleia's a big surprise.
Why is it that the one I have
is shunned by all the butterflies?

The garden books all say they love it.
They seem to hate the one outside.
They love a buddleia elsewhere,
but mine, alas, they can't abide.

Some friends say it's the scent I wear.
Could that be why they never stay?
What makes them hate my buddleia?
What makes them always soar away?

Perhaps it's not my buddleia.
Perhaps it's just the sight of me
that scares the butterflies away.
I'd love to solve the mystery.

Vegetable garden

I picture folk who stroll outside
and bring in home-grown lettuces,
and turnips, spuds and cabbages
and baskets full of strawberries.

Ah, how I'd love to go outside
and pick a raspberry or two,
or loads of them to make a tart –
that's something I'd so love to do !

How wonderful to stroll outside
when feeling that I'd like a snack,
and pluck a carrot from the earth
or bring a tasty radish back!

I'd love to have a patch like that,
but sadly, do not have the space.
Do you? Then you may sometimes see
a touch of envy on my face.

My Mr Gatsby

The problem was, I loved your garden,
but sadly, didn't love you too –
well, not as much, and not enough.
I knew I couldn't marry you.

I loved the rhododendron drive,
the statues and the topiary.
I loved the cedars on the lawn.
You loved them too, and you loved me.

I loved the gorgeous lily pond,
a thousand blossoms floating there!
I loved the kitchen garden too –
your own fresh produce everywhere.

I loved the greenhouse – what a dream,
with loads of overhanging vines,
and what is more, enough of them
to make your own delicious wines.

I loved the banks of lavender –
a mass of them, a stunning show,
and gazing at the roses there
while sitting on your patio.

The love affair was not to be.
I loved your garden, that was true –
but never loved you quite as much –
that's something that I couldn't do.

And what a crying shame that was –
to love your garden with a passion,
and love it so much more than you,
and not, alas, in equal ration.

A botanist puts me right

'Dandelions? A thousand types.'
(And I thought there was only one).
'You're not alone in thinking that.
Well, so does almost everyone.
A thousand different variations –
we're always finding something new.
The dandelion is most surprising.'

'A thousand types? That can't be true!'

'Wait there, my dear' – he potters off
returning with a heavy book.
I marvel at its size and weight,
and, quite astonished, take a look.

'You see, my dear, all kinds of them,
and every single one keeps changing,
not quite content to stay that way,
and somewhere, somehow, rearranging.'

They all looked much the same to me –
the dandelions that filled the pages.
I gave the volume back to him.
To read it would have taken ages.

'You see my dear, a thousand types,
and you imagined only one?
But I'll forgive your ignorance.
You're pretty much like everyone.'

I wander happy, not a cloud

I wander happy, not a cloud
above me in the summer sun,
at last, with warmer days allowed
to get out there and get things done,
to plant and tend things, see things grow
and then sit back and watch the show.

I wander in the summer breeze
rejoicing that the season's here,
while gentle breezes rustle trees
and buds and blooms and shoots appear.
Each day a lovely new surprise
to lift my spirits, thrill my eyes.

The border springs, the robin sings,
the grass is growing, growing, growing.
I'm pruning things and tending things
and humming while I do the mowing,
and often out at early dawn
to pluck a weed upon the lawn.

Quite oft, when on my couch I lie
in happy and contented mood,
they flash upon my inward eye –
those wintry days of servitude.
There's ne'er a reason now to sigh,
the sun so high within the sky.

Robin

I love it when you sing to me.
I love your chirpy gaiety.
I love it when you sing to me –
it helps me live contentedly.

I love the way, when I am weeding,
you take a moment off from feeding
to thrill me with your heartfelt song,
as if, somehow, we two belong.

You comfort me when you are singing.
Sing on, sing on, each time you're bringing
more restful thoughts into my mind
and helping tension to unwind.

My god-daughter Sophie – another true story

Sophie couldn't say her 'r's'–
a charming lisp, and lucky too;
it gave the child a love of flowers.
It's lovely what a lisp can do!

At school, when asked what she enjoyed,
she told the teacher, 'I like weeding!'
Of course, what Sophie meant to say
was what she liked to do was reading.

Then, given a small plot to weed,
she did just that for many hours,
and after that, she planted it
and ended up with loads of flowers.

And these days, now three decades on,
she still loves gardening (even weeding),
and all because she couldn't say
the starting letter 'r' in reading.

AUTUMN

Season of strolls, in woodlands now ablaze
with hues of fiery red and stunning gold

Autumn

Season of strolls, in woodlands now ablaze
with hues of fiery red and stunning gold.
Season of mists, and hazy golden days
announcing that the year is growing old.
Season of exhaustion – endless raking
and piles of soggy leaves on which to slip,
and sitting in the traffic while you're taking
another load to throw into the skip.
Season of tossed trees and leaves a-flying,
and watching plants start sighing, crying, dying,
despite the valiant efforts you are making.

Pieris forestii

My pieris – on fire again.
Fabulous! A sheet of flame!
But what a crying shame it is
it makes its neighbours look so tame.
Nothing else within the garden
gives quite the same bright blaze of red.
I think I'll pull your neighbours out
and plant more pieris instead.

Autumn years

Remember all those daisies growing
before they disappeared with mowing,
and putting on a daisy chain?

Few children ever will again.

Remember shelling garden peas?
('We don't want any maggots, please!')
and maggot races at your school?

What children now would think that cool?

Remember, when you were a child,
exploring – often on your own.
What mother would allow that now?

What child would ever go alone?

Remember having a 'veranda'
before you called it 'patio' –
that wasn't floored with wooden decking?

It seems a million years ago.

Remember frost on window panes
when waking in the freezing cold,
in shapes of graceful ferns and flowers?

You do? Like me, you're getting old.

Thorpeness, Suffolk

Years ago, on Thorpeness cliffs
I gathered mushrooms by the score.
I'd take a basket, fill it up,
until I couldn't fit in more.
And one dawn, I was even able
to cover half a ping pong table
with mushrooms picked upon my way.
But where have they all gone today?
Perhaps it is the huge reactor
put up near Thorpeness years ago.
Is something in there changing things?
Is that why mushrooms do not grow
in thousands like they used to do?
I dearly hope that isn't true.

Sod's Law

You stroll around a neighbour's garden
and spot a plant you'd like to grow.
Of course you've picked the very one
whose name your neighbour doesn't know.

'Hang on a second. No, that's wrong.
But wait, it might just come to me.'
You do, you wait, but does it come?
You stand there, waiting patiently.

'It's coming to me! No, it's not.
I'm sorry, but I've quite forgotten.
I used to know its name so well.
My memory is going rotten!'

You snip a bit and take it home,
and then consult your books alone.
But can you ever find the plant?
It's not in any books you own.

The more you like your neighbour's plant,
the less chance she will know its name,
or you will find it back at home.
Sod's law – it's always just the same.

The garden centre

I know just what I want to buy,
and know it's at the centre,
but then I always change my mind
immediately I enter.

I spot a plant not on my list,
and know I have to own it,
despite the fact it's new to me
and I have never grown it.

And then it goes and dies on me,
or else does something funny.
I must stick to my list next time –
again I've wasted money.

Too late to get the other plant
and for the simplest reason –
the planting time has been and gone.
It's too late in the season.

'My garden has to be tidy'

A neighbour once said that to me.
I didn't say 'I disagree'.
Instead, I said, 'I must confess
to liking bits of wilderness.'

I love things rambling everywhere
and one or two surprises there,
with wild things springing up from seed.
Indeed, I often like a weed.

He liked his plants kept neat and low –
to me, an uninspiring show.
The place was always neat and trim,
or else it irritated him.

The lawn? He'd so perfected it,
you weren't allowed to walk on it.
I never was allowed to go
much further than his patio.

And this was quite beyond belief –
you never saw a single leaf
upon that swathe of green perfection
or weed that had escaped detection.

He peered at my place through the fence:
'I'm sorry, I mean no offence,
but don't you want to tidy it
and take the garden back a bit?'

I didn't. Tidy's not for me.
We both agreed to disagree,
untidy me, and tidy he,
and lived next door quite affably.

Leaves me cold

Autumn in the woods is one thing,
but in my garden, what a bore.
Each day at dawn I look outside
and see the leaves, a whole lot more,
and feel my disposition sagging.
I can't face all that endless bagging
and driving to the council skip –
it's far too much for just one trip.
I love the colours – bright and bold –
the flaming red and stunning gold,
but not the sweeping, now I'm old.
I have to say, that leaves me cold.

I wander lonely as a cloud

I wander lonely as a cloud
around my garden, now a mess.
The only tasks that I'm allowed
are those that bore me, bring distress.
I wander, angry, mood now black
to fill another plastic sack.

All clearing, brushing, raking, hoeing
and digging every flowerbed
with very little out there growing,
and wilting, dying there instead.
By twelve o'clock I need a gin
to cope with all the mess it's in.

Ten bags now piled outside the door,
I've not the strength to do much more.
The awful state the garden's in
now tempts me in to drink that gin
and give up, angry, mood now bleak;
I cannot face another week.

Quite oft when on my couch I lie
in sorry mood and feeling blue,
I think of rubbish sacks out there –
and all the rest I've got to do.
I cannot face another leaf –
so many, it's beyond belief.

With apologies to William Wordsworth

Elderflower

A wine buff came to dinner –
a chap called Cyril Ray,
an expert on the subject
(and sadly, dead today).

We served a splendid claret –
a name among the best,
and happily he loved it
and seemed to be impressed.

And then, for the dessert course,
we changed to something white,
and watched old Cyril beaming –
'I'm glad I came tonight!

My favourite! Chateau d'Yquem!
How very kind of you!'
But was it Chateau d'Yquem?
Er, no, that wasn't true.

Our choice was far more humble –
our home-made elderflower,
but Cyril sat there beaming
at least another hour.

He studied it, the bottle,
surprised to see no label,
and sighed when it was empty
and taken from the table.

And then my husband blew it
(a much too honest bloke),
and sadly poor old Cyril
did not enjoy the joke.

'It's elderflower, Cyril!
It grows out in the garden!'
Disaster – he was livid.
We watched his visage harden.

He had a reputation –
an expert, he was vain,
and promptly left the table
and never came again.

*(This is a true story, although the home-made elderflower wine
wasn't served by my husband, but by my father-in-law, the wicked
Toby O'Brien, fond of a practical joke. Cyril Ray was a
famous wine writer for The Sunday Times, but was obviously
caught out on occasions).*

The pond

A heron flew in, spiked a fish
and then it gobbled up another.
We used to have six goldfish there.
All dead. We'll never have another.

Nature's lovely in the wild,
but rather less so in the raw,
and when it visits you like that,
you wonder what you loved it for.

'Have you noticed?'

'Have you noticed our hydrangea?'
'Where?'
'Oh darling, by the door!'
'The white thing?'
'No, the pink thing, darling.'
'Why should I notice it?
What for?'

'I'm worried that our cherry tree
has some disease. It's slowly dying.'
'The cherry tree? Which one is that?'
I tell him, though I feel like crying.

'I think I'd like some rhododendrons.
The colour would look lovely here.'
'Remind me; what are rhododendrons?'
You sigh, and shed another tear.

You love the garden, he may not,
but loves the fact that you do though.
So you forgive his ignorance
and all the plants he doesn't know.

Gladioli

Gladioli? Not a favourite.
At times, I sometimes wonder why.
I see the bulbs in garden centres
and every time I walk on by.

Perhaps because when I was young
hairdressers used to love them so.
A vase was always in their windows
some fifty, sixty years ago.

And back then, kids had 'pudding basins',
a cut so ugly, truly vile.
Hairdressers were a dreaded place
for kids who had an ounce of style.

Some memories stop you growing flowers
you might have chosen otherwise.
What other people rave about
you find offensive to you eyes.

Bryology

It's pretty easy understanding
why people like biology,
but why would someone ever want
to go into bryology?

Professionals who study moss
and nothing else, their whole profession?
It's true that several people do –
but what a strange and odd obsession!

How can they study only moss,
and make the stuff their whole career?
It leaves me at a total loss
when scraping off the moss round here.

To study mosses all year round
and never see a single flower?
And do the same, day in, day out?
I'd last for only half an hour.

But then, I'm pretty ignorant.
I hardly even know what moss is.
I'm simply not that interested,
and don't count moss among my losses.

And what is more astonishing –
not one bryologist can cope
or study any moss at all
unless they use a microscope.
Topology, biology, dendrology, cytology –
of all the 'ologies' I know, the oddest is bryology.

Bloody neighbour

Virginia creeper – wonderful –
backbreaking during winter though.
It seems to shed a million leaves,
far more than any plant I know.

The one on our house went and died.
And I know how. I'm sure I know.
Our next door neighbour hated it
and killed it off five years ago.

I loved that creeper on our house
despite the mass of leaves to clear.
Our neighbour hated all the mess
and couldn't stand it being here.

She painted on a chemical,
it only took a leaf or two
to kill the rest, and in a year.
Oh, what a dreadful thing to do!

I watched it die from tips to roots –
the way systemics always kill.
The cause of death was obvious.
It wasn't that the plant was ill.

Virginia creeper – glorious –
a blaze of colour every year.
My neighbour's thrilled she killed it off –
that's why I don't invite her here.

Garden statuary

My sister likes pigs,
the other loves frogs,
I'm fond of a cherub or two.
My brother likes pots,
and better still, lots,
and must have a fountain on view.

My neighbour loves gods
and classical bods
like Venus and Sappho and Mars.
Another likes rocks
with gizmos within
that pick up the light from the stars.

And some like to own
a birdbath in stone,
or something attached to a wall –
a few heads perhaps,
of mythical chaps.
And some folk like nothing at all.

But millions love gnomes
surrounding their homes,
and find them a huge satisfaction.
What is it with gnomes?
It fascinates me.
What is it about their attraction?

Wildly ignorant

What dog gave us Dog's Mercury?
What gypsy, Gypsywort?
Did shepherds carry purses
and pee on Bladderwort?

Do geese like eating Gooseberries?
Do Cowslips make cows slip?
(They're pretty bulky creatures,
I've never seen one trip).

Did seamstresses name Stitchwort?
Does Sneezewort make you sneeze?
Do horses eat Horseradish?
What's sweet about Sweet Peas?

What lizard named an Orchid?
Did Solomon name Seals?
Were Baneberries annoying?
Was Cudweed cattle meals?

What puss loved Pussywillow?
Are Catkins liked by cats?
What dame named the Dame's Violet?
Was Mat Grass used for mats?

And who was Ragged Robin?
Is Fleabane where fleas meet?
Who wore the Lady's Mantle,
and what makes Meadowsweet?

Did lovers say 'Forget me not'
if forced to live apart?
And did they then use Heartsease
to mend a broken heart?

So many, many questions –
an ignoramus, me.
Who named our native species,
and so confusingly?

A bet

While dining out we placed a bet,
and one that I will not forget:
one hundred wild flowers jotted down
before we drove away from town.

He laughed at me, and shook his head.
'I bet you can't do that', he said.
'I think I can' was my reply.
But could I? It was worth a try.

I took a paper serviette,
deciding to take up the bet.
He watched me scribbling, fascinated,
and then for twenty minutes waited.

I thought of every plant and weed –
he never thought that I'd succeed.
One hundred pounds was quite a sum –
I hoped a hundred names would come.

They did, with memories on my side
of every lovely cycle ride
from six years old until eleven
when hedgerows passed were utter heaven.

Just twenty minutes, not an hour,
recalling every single flower
I cycled past, and every day –
the wild ones you don't see today.

I won. He paid, and all was square,
and then, when driving off from there,
I realized it could take hours
or stretch beyond most people's powers
recalling those same flowers today –
long-gone beneath a motorway.

Memories of my mother

Admiring your geraniums
in pots around your patio;
bringing flowers into the house –
you always had a vase on show;

strolling with your walking stick
and poking, thrusting as you go,
pushing ferns and twigs aside
to see the primroses below;

planting baby cyclamens
and dotting them around the drive.
'I think it's nice for visitors
to see them here when they arrive';

clipping things and snipping things,
and never leaving things 'til later,
and melting your engagement ring.
And how? In the incinerator;

parking on a motorway –
incredibly, right on the shoulder.
And why? To pick some cowslips there.
It's fortunate that you grew older;

clearing leaves and burning them,
and 'til the end, the task of mowing
the croquet lawn that stretched outside,
and keeping house and garden going.

So many memories live on –
they soothe me, now that you have gone.

WINTER

Don't want your pond to freeze right over?
Just float a tennis ball on top

Winter

Season of snow, and frost and bitterness
and hardened earth, and weak and struggling sun,
with days of grey to cloud your happiness
and bring you thoughts of all you haven't done.
More leaves to clear upon the sodden lawn –
a task, each year, that fills your heart with dread,
within a garden now so bleak, forlorn,
where everything is dormant, dull or dead,
and nothing is in bloom and few birds sing.
You do not have the will to do a thing
until the sun arrives when spring is born.

With apologies to John Keats

Wandering off again

I wandered miserable as sin
around the garden, bleak and bare,
and cried to see the state within
with plants and flowers dying there –
within the borders, round the trees,
no blossoms blowing in the breeze.

Continuous as the stars that shine
and twinkle as the milky way
there stood a never-ending line
of plants once gorgeous, dead today.
Two hundred saw I at a glance,
not tossing now in sprightly dance.

The wind beside them danced, but they
no longer bobbed and pranced in glee,
as all of them had passed away –
gone, all that jocund company.
I gazed, I cried, and sadly thought –
the flowering season's all too short.

Quite oft, when on my couch I lie
in vacant and in pensive mood,
they flash upon my inward eye
and spoil my winter solitude.
And then my heart with sadness fills.
I'll have to wait for daffodils.

You wandered lonely as a cloud,
but happy, wandering in Spring.
I wandered out in Wintertime,
and didn't see a blooming thing
except the work I had to do –
I felt depressed, so unlike you.

Apologies again to William Wordsworth

You're all rotters

A plastic pot will never rot,
but how much nicer, terracotta,
until it cracks and chips a lot –
in winter it's a dreadful rotter.

A plastic pot is somewhat vulgar,
and how much nicer, terracotta.
But still, I don't like cracks and chips
to look at when it's getting hotter.

Alas, a good pot rarely lasts,
so many of them crack and splinter.
I love a pot in terracotta,
but few of them will last a winter.

A plastic pot is rather crude,
and cannot ever look fantastic
despite the plant that grows inside.
But what do you expect from plastic?

No-one likes such pots a lot.
Nor me, but buy them as they last,
fed up with terracotta ones
that failed me in the winters past.

Plastic pots now fill my garden,
and all of them look rather grotty,
but still, I'm tired of terracotta,
it always cracks and drives me potty.

Poinsettias

Poinsettias – such ugly sisters.
For me, they always spoil the ball.
Why is it every Christmastime
we feel we should invite them all?

Poinsettias – that Christmas plant,
an annual necessity.
Each year, I'm always given one,
and sometimes, even two or three.

Poinsettias, they're not for me,
but still I stick one in the hall,
and then groan when the heating's on
and all their bracts begin to fall.

A potting shed

I have a wish before I'm dead –
to have a decent potting shed.
I have a shed, oh yes, I know,
but filled with junk from years ago
my husband doesn't want to throw,
yet things he doesn't need again –
a hoarder, like so many men.
I'd love a shed before I go,
but won't. A hopeless wish, I know.

I have a wish before I'm dead –
to have a decent potting shed.
I'll never have one, yes I know,
well, not unless we up and go
to somewhere with a bigger space
where I can have a potting place.
But move? We'd hate it, that I know.
We'll never move, we'll never go,
and even if we had two sheds
he'd use both for his overflow.

Mary and her secret garden

Her own private wilderness –
haven of peacefulness –
a garden that only she knows;
a place of sheer heaven
if aged around seven,
where nobody else ever goes.

A garden that's secret,
where roses are rambling
and wild things can easily grow;
with only one key to it
so she can see to it
no other person can go.

When Mary is yearning
for peace, and she's turning
that solitary key in the door,
the problems stay outside
as soon as she's inside –
or don't seem as bad any more.

Imagine – a wilderness,
a wildness, a quietness,
a garden that's only for you.
I'd find that pure heaven
like Mary at seven.
I dreamed of it once, and still do.

Groan

The mower's gone all rusty,
the chestnut tree needs lopping –
the crown is now gigantic;
a third of it needs chopping.

The garden door is rotting
and flopping on its hinges,
and always blowing open –
another of my whinges.

The lawn is looking dreadful,
great patches need reseeding,
and as for all the flowerbeds,
the whole damned lot need weeding.

The pond is black and filthy,
the lilies are in trouble,
they'll die if I don't dredge it,
and do it at the double.

The walls are falling over,
the neighbour's new extension
has ruined all our pointing –
another cause of tension.

The statue's fallen over –
the cherub's now beheaded.
But how on earth to fix it?
Another task I've dreaded.

Everything needs doing,
my mood is growing black,
and lifting up the statue
has now done in my back.

A house can be exhausting,
a garden even more,
and though I love it most times,
it's frequently a bore.

Rubbish

Of course, all households need a bin
to put the junk and rubbish in,
or two or three, or sometimes more –
an ugly sight outside the door
or sitting somewhere in the drive –
first thing guests see when they arrive.
But what are we supposed to do
to hide the things, improve the view?

It may come as a nice surprise
that cupboards are a great disguise.
It doesn't take a lot of wit,
but most folk never think of it.
A lovely cupboard made of wood
could make your entrance look so good!
An ugly sight – a rubbish bin.
A cupboard's what it should be in.

Viagra

Splendid perk-up for cut flowers
when wilting, tilting, falling ill –
simply feed them with Viagra.
Crush up a quarter of a pill.

Drop it in the vase that evening,
then go to bed and sleep for hours
(or not, if you have got Viagra)
and in the morning, see your flowers!

All at once they're standing upright,
not flopping, drooping as before.
You've got Viagra in the house?
Another thing to use it for.

My friend Tricia

She loves inviting friends around,
they're always round there for a drink,
with little things to nibble on
that disappear within a wink.

And what a noisy bunch they are!
They love to chatter and to sing,
and keep her entertained for hours
while drinking, eating everything.

There's always someone winging in,
and always a great welcome there.
I've never seen that many birds –
she never leaves their table bare.

Abraham Cowley

An ancestor, Abraham Cowley,
wrote poems far better than me.
There's one he once wrote in a garden –
it hangs in our WC.

I thought that you might like to read it –
it's always a comfort to me.
I think it expresses exactly
how life and how gardens should be.

Ah, yet

Ah, yet e'er I descend to the grave
may I a small house
and large garden have!
And a few friends, and many books,
both true,
both wise and both delightful too!
And since love ne'er will from me flee,
a partner moderately fair,
and good as guardian angels are,
only belov'd, and loving me.

Abraham Cowley, 1618–1667

Floating quiche tins

Ever seen a floating quiche tin?
If not, then pop along to Kew
and stroll around the lily house –
you'll find a mass of them on view.

Each lily pad that floats in there
reminds me of a baking tin –
round, flat, and with a frilly edge –
like those you bake your quiches in.

A pond of giant, floating quiche tins
to marvel at and make you smile –
a splendid thing to view at Kew
and make a visit worth your while.

I find each pad quite fascinating
as many other women do,
and no-one ever leaves the place
without a photograph or two.

Holly

What's the point of growing holly?
Whatever do I have it for?
It's merry with its berries on,
but that's a month or so, no more.

What's the point of having holly?
To make a wreath outside the door,
and only do that once a year?
What else do I have holly for?

What's the point of growing holly?
To jolly up the house a bit,
and then see all the berries fall
and make a bloody mess of it?

I think I'll take the shears to it.
It's far too big, I know I should.
I only need a tiny sprig
to pop upon the Christmas pud.

A garden graveyard

When Grandma's dogs had passed away
she buried them with crosses,
and sighed 'Until a dog has died,
you don't know what a loss is.'

Her garden had ten crosses there,
and when she tended flowers
she thought about her furry friends
and all their happy hours.

And every time I visited
I said a little prayer,
while reading names on every cross
within the graveyard there.

The first time visiting their plot
I even shed a tear
when reading what was on the gate –
'Let sleeping dogs lie here'.

Demented

Without some kind of space outside
to grow a plant or two,
I know that I would soon go mad –
before a month was through.

But millions do exactly that,
and seem to be contented,
a mystery to the rest of us
who'd soon become demented.

A patio, a tiny yard,
a space however small,
would serve to keep my spirits up.
But have no space at all?

I guess a ledge, a window sill
would then have to suffice,
but soon I think my mental state
would start to pay the price.

Tennis ball

Don't want your pond to freeze all over?
Just float a tennis ball on top.
That leaves an air hole on the surface.
No more to say, so now I'll stop.

Inside in my dressing gown

Too cold to step outside now –
there's frost upon the grass.
I'll stay here in the kitchen
and let the winter pass.

Too cold to venture outside
and wander round at dawn.
I'll stay here in the kitchen
until the spring is born.

Mistletoe

The guests you don't feel much like kissing –
why is it they're the first to go
and stand precisely where you've hung
your bunch of Christmas mistletoe?

Christmas, what have I done?

Most gardeners look back on the year
reflecting on the things they've done
to make their patch a nicer place
when blessed with light and hours of sun.

And older ones may well reflect –
well, if they are at all like me,
that things may go downhill from now
with sagging, failing energy.

But then, the Springtime comes again.
And once again, we're out there thinking
'Now, what to plant or change this year?'
And suddenly our hearts stop sinking!

Mid January

With Christmas trees the streets are strewn,
so many I've stopped counting –
at least a hundred down our road,
and numbers keep on mounting.

How sad to see those Christmas trees
whenever going shopping.
I sigh to think how many die
in all those weeks of chopping.

How sad to see those Christmas trees –
so lovely once when growing.
How sad to see them on our streets,
the pavements overflowing.

The rubbish trucks are here quite soon,
with blades for quick compressing.
Quite soon they'll be a pile of sludge –
I find the thought depressing.

Pine needles too, all round the house,
and brushing up is wearing.
So many of them everywhere,
so many I'm despairing.

The legacy of plants

Plants can plant a love within you
 that sometimes lasts you all life long.
At times you may reflect on that
when nurturing new plants along.
Plants can plant a love within you
that stays until your very last,
and often leaves good memories
for those reflecting on your past.
They'll picture you within your garden
while pottering contentedly,
and maybe in your dressing gown –
that's if you are at all like me.

A happy ending

I pulled a rosebush out last year
and fractured a left rib,
and toppled down the steps this year
and smashed my tib and fib.

The year before I broke my wrist
when lifting up a pot,
and promptly tumbling over it.
That also hurt a lot.

That's not to count the bites and stings
from ants and wasps and spiders.
It's far more safe to stay away
like sensible insiders.

For five months, I've been wheelchair-bound.
Will I go out again?
Of course I will, I'm just like you –
most gardeners are insane.

We fall off ladders on our backs,
and lose our toes when mowing –
that's if we use machines that float
and don't look where we're going.

We soon forget where hosepipes are
and trip up on the grass,
and risk our hips with silly slips
each time we try and pass.

We poke our eyes on bamboo sticks
that somehow miss our vision,
and risk our lives attempting things
we've seen on television.

A garden is a dangerous place.
But keep out? I won't ever.
Of course, it is a danger zone,
but keep out? Never! Never!

Like other folk, I'd rather die
while sleeping in my bed.
The chances are, I'll meet my end
when gardening instead.

Gardeners have the last word

Of course we do –'the seeds of doubt',
'digging up old history',
'raking up old grievances',
'green shoots of recovery.'

'Planting thoughts in someone's head',
'a budding talent', 'flower of youth',
'turning over a new leaf',
'digging deep to get the truth.'

'Sowing wild oats' in our youth,
'tree of knowledge',' forking out',
'going back to one's old roots',
'mown down', 'rooted', 'weeded out.'

'Led right up the garden path',
'rooted in our history',
'down to earth' and 'going green'.
You're crazy! 'You are off your tree!'

'Getting to the root of things'.
You've just 'unearthed' a great idea,
but one they then 'nip in the bud.'
'It's never going 'to bear fruit' here.

'Wallflowers', never asked to dance.
'Life is not a bed of roses'.
'A wilting violet', 'English rose' –
how very flowery English prose is!

'No stone unturned', 'the primrose path',
'the flowering of a genius',
'our Autumn years', 'the rites of Spring'–
all sayings so well known to us.

Quite stupendous? 'Blooming marvellous!'
'Blossoming into old age',
'rosy' cheeks in wintertime,
a 'budding' star upon the stage.

Gardening's rooted in our language.
Quite often it amazes me
how many gardening turns of phrase
have entered our vocabulary.

'Gone to seed' – that rude expression.
'You're on my turf – please go away!'
'The grass is greener' – it's so true
we gardeners *do* have the last say!